The Dying of Jesus

The Dying of Jesus

Words and Thoughts from the Cross

Owen F. Cummings

Foreword by John C. Wester

CASCADE *Books* · Eugene, Oregon

THE DYING OF JESUS
Words and Thoughts from the Cross

Cascade Books
An Imprint of Wipf and Stock Publishers
199 W. 8th Ave., Suite 3
Eugene, OR 97401

www.wipfandstock.com

PAPERBACK ISBN: 978-1-4982-3816-8
HARDCOVER ISBN: 978-1-4982-3818-2
EBOOK ISBN: 978-1-4982-3817-5

Cataloguing-in-Publication data:

Names: Cummings, Owen F. | Wester, John C., foreword.

Title: The dying of Jesus : words and thoughts from the cross / Owen F.
Cummings ; foreword by John C. Wester.

Description: Eugene, OR : Cascade Books, 2016 | Includes biblio-
graphical references.

Identifiers: ISBN 978-1-4982-3816-8 (paperback) | ISBN 978-1-4982-
3818-2 (hardcover) | ISBN 978-1-4982-3817-5 (ebook)

Subjects: LCSH: Jesus Christ—Seven last words—Meditations.

Classification: BT457 .C86 2016 (paperback) | BT457 .C86 (ebook)

Manufactured in the U.S.A.   07/07/16

In memory of

Amos House

and

Fr. Paschal Cheline, OSB

Contents

Foreword

Deacon Owen F. Cummings has done it again! This gifted writer, with his singular grasp of the English language, has written a fresh and captivating reflection on Christ's final thoughts from the cross. His clear and insightful approach to the traditional Good Friday theme of the "Seven Last Words" is based on solid theology, sound spirituality, cogent scriptural insight and a mature understanding of the human heart. I have been impressed over the years with Deacon Cummings' facility in writing about such diverse topics as liturgy, comparative religion, ministry in today's church, spirituality, and systematic theology. Yet, what emerges from these pages is not only the product of a gifted scholar but also the insights of a man close to the Lord with a facility for speaking to people's lives, whether in the seminary classroom or the parish church. While anyone's last words are certainly compelling, this is even more the case when it comes to our Savior himself. What a gift that although Jesus had the "last words" from the cross several thousand years ago, we can still ponder their echo in this gem of a book.

The Most Reverend John C. Wester
Archbishop of Santa Fe

Introduction

The Dying of Jesus: Words and Thoughts from the Cross came to birth in St. James Cathedral, Seattle, on Good Friday, 2015. The pastor of the cathedral, Fr. Michael G. Ryan, invited me to present the series of Good Friday meditations on "The Seven Last Words of Jesus." I shall never forget the solemn beauty of the cathedral and the immense care with which the three-hour service was designed, combining Scripture, meditation, and music. It was a great honor to be invited, and it was a very moving spiritual experience for me. My thanks go to Fr. Ryan for his great kindness and generosity, and through him to the people who assembled in the cathedral on Good Friday; and also to Maria Laughlin, assistant to Fr. Ryan, who did so much to smooth the way for me to be present on that memorable day.

(Deacon) Owen F. Cummings
Academic Dean and Regents' Professor of Theology
Mount Angel Seminary

1

The Sign of the Cross

The cross is the defining image of Christianity. The cross by itself, or as a *crucifix* with a depiction of the body of Christ fastened to it, is found in countless places: mounted on church steeples, embroidered on sacred vestments, attached to the walls of homes and institutions, tattooed on the hands of Coptic monks, fashioned into jewelry worn by believers as a symbol of their faith and by others merely as an exotic necklace or earring.

—Donald Senior[1]

1. Senior, *Why the Cross?*, xiii.

DEATH BY CRUCIFIXION FOR JEWS, CHRISTIANS, AND MUSLIMS

The earliest Christians had to react to the death of Jesus particularly because it was a real stumbling block for them, what they called a "scandal," and this reaction may have been expressed in what many regard as the origins of the gospels, that is, the passion narrative. Many scholars think that the passion narrative developed fairly quickly as a kind of apologetic for the crucifixion. We read in 1 Cor 1:23, "But we proclaim Christ crucified, a stumbling block to Jews and foolishness to Gentiles." The word for "stumbling block" is the Greek word *skandalon*, and the word for "foolishness" is the Greek word *moria*, the root from which "moron" comes. So, the cross of Jesus was something you might stumble over for the Jews, and for the Gentiles something that only a fool could believe that God was positively involved. To the Jews, talk of a crucified messiah must have seemed blasphemous on the basis of Deut 21:22–23: "If a man guilty of a capital offense is put to death and his corpse hung on a tree, it shall not remain on the tree overnight. You shall bury it the same day; otherwise, since God's curse rests on him who hangs upon a tree, you will defile the land which the LORD, your God, is giving you as an inheritance." Being "hanged upon a tree" was interpreted in first-century Palestinian Judaism as being crucified. Since Jesus was crucified, God's curse must have rested upon him. The stumbling block for Jews was obvious. "The Messiah of Israel could never ever at the same time be the one who according to the words of the Torah was accursed by God."[2] Some response to this

2. Hengel, *Atonement*, 43.

apparent absurdity had to be made, and not only for the Jewish element in early Christianity. To Gentile ears, the crucifixion, preached as a saving event, in some way, shape, or form beneficial for human beings, must not have been less absurd. That a man dying in such a repulsive fashion could have anything to do with the divine world was utter foolishness, and something only a "moron" could believe.

This moronic attitude is expressed in what has come to be known as the graffito of Alexamenos. This graffito was scratched in plaster in Rome circa 200 AD. It shows a crucified man with the head of an ass. Next to him is a smaller figure named Alexamenos, who has his arm extended toward the crucified. Nearby the following words are etched: "Alexamenos worships [his] God." It seems clearly to be the case that Alexamenos was a Christian and some crude artist has shown in the graffito what he thinks of Alexamenos's god, the crucified Jesus. The graffito expresses what St. Paul means by "foolishness" from a pagan Gentile point of view. How could any right-minded person believe that God was somehow active in the death of a crucified man? The comment of theologian Richard Viladesau is helpful: "It is the earliest known pictorial representation of the crucifixion of Christ and of his adoration as divine. In a city so full of the triumphant monuments of Christianity, there is something strangely moving in finding this first visual testimony to the Christian faith amidst the fragments of daily life of pagan Rome; and even more so in finding it in this rude sketch, probably drawn by a palace page with cruel schoolboy humor to mock the faith of a fellow slave."[3]

3. Viladesau, *Beauty of the Cross*, 19.

The scandal of the cross remains a scandal also for devout Muslims. In his book on the cross, Viladesau goes on to share an experience from his teaching at Fordham University in New York. Christian students in one of his classes were utterly surprised at the reverence that Muslims had for the person of Jesus, "and even more surprised that most Muslims teach that Jesus was not crucified." Viladesau asked a Muslim student to explain this idea that Jesus was not crucified to the rest of the class; here is the gist of her response: "It is inconceivable that God should allow his Prophet and Messiah to suffer such a death; rather, God took Jesus to himself (See Koran 4.157–58)." At that time, Mel Gibson's movie *The Passion of the Christ* was attracting a large number of moviegoers; Vildesau reports that "another Muslim student commented that while he was very affected by the portrayal of human suffering in Mel Gibson's film on the passion, he obviously could not believe that any of this had happened to the Christ: either it happened to someone else, or it was an illusion produced by God."[4] So, the cross has been a scandal, foolishness—or, because of God's concern for Jesus, it never really took place.

THE SIGN OF THE CROSS

The image of Christ on the cross was a latecomer in Christian religious expression. The specialists tell us that the earliest surviving examples of Christ on the cross date from the fifth century. It is pointed out that the earlier image of the Good Shepherd, found often in the catacombs and

4. Ibid., 7–8.

represented in early Christian sculpture, was a more attractive and consoling image for early Christians. The image of the Good Shepherd depicts Jesus's dedication and sacrifice, his willingness to die for his flock, as in John 10:11: "I am the good shepherd. The good shepherd lays down his life for the sheep." The image of Christ as the Good Shepherd does not show him suffering. In point of fact, many of the earliest Christian images of the cross do not show a crucified and suffering Christ. "Either: they show only his head, or they show him glorious and triumphant, rather than in agony, wearing the tunic of a Byzantine emperor, or a purple royal or priestly robe. Early Christian artists tended to avoid depicting Christ as dead, on the Cross or elsewhere."[5] Historians of art may present various reasons for this, but surely one reason stands out from our human point of view. Suffering is difficult to reconcile with the understanding of God as Love. The image of the Good Shepherd in its own way seems to convey this so much better. Later generations of Christians were to develop different and sometimes challenging ways of thinking about the suffering of Christ on the cross, but surely all have come to recognize that Jesus did not come to placate an angry God, nor to be a model for submission to a cruel God. "He came to be the love of God; to show in our own 'frail flesh' not what God demands but what God is prepared to give."[6] "He came to be the love of God"—that is the whole point of the incarnation and of the cross—to manifest to us what it means when we say that God is Love (1 John 4:16), and in and through that manifestation gracefully to embrace us in the communion of the Trinity. Whether intended or

5. Sherry, *Images of Redemption*, 66.
6. Barton, *Love Unknown*, 4.

not, there is a firm strand of at least Western theological thought about the cross that sees it in terms of punishment. Perhaps this strand of punishment thinking reveals something unsavory about ourselves, but it certainly does not reveal the Trinitarian God whose best name is Love.[7]

A couple of references to early Christian writers help us to see how precious the sign of the cross had become. Our first author is Tertullian (ca. 160–ca. 225), a Christian from Carthage in North Africa. Around the year 211, he wrote a book entitled *De Corona* (*Concerning the Crown*), in which he commends a Roman soldier for refusing to wear the soldier's crown. Tertullian believed the crown to be a symbol of paganism, and he was utterly opposed to it.[8] Tertullian contrasts the pagan symbol with the sign of the cross: "At every forward step and movement, at every going in and out, when we put on our clothes and shoes, when we bathe, when we sit at table, when we light the lamps, on couch, on seat, in all the ordinary actions of daily life, we trace upon the forehead the sign."[9] Tertullian was writing while Christianity was still an illicit religion and persecutions occurred. That was not the case with our second example, Cyril of Jerusalem (ca. 315–86). Cyril lived in the century after the Edict of Milan, when peace came to the church, free of persecution, under the Roman emperor Constantine. We know a great deal about the early church's liturgy from Cyril, as well as about Jerusalem as a holy place and a growing center of pilgrimage, but he also offers us this engaging passage about the sign of the cross: "Let us then not be ashamed to confess the Crucified. Let

7. Hauerwas, *Cross-Shattered Christ*, 29–30.

8. Cross, *Early Christian Fathers*, 145.

9. Tertullian, *De Corona*, ch. 3.

the Cross, as our seal, be boldly made with our fingers upon our brow, and on all occasions; over the bread we eat, over the cups we drink; in our comings and in our goings; before sleep; on lying down and rising up; when we are on the way and when we are still. It is a powerful safeguard; it is without price, for the sake of the poor; without toil, because of the sick; for it is a grace from God, a badge of the faithful, and a terror to the devils; for 'he displayed them openly, leading them away in triumph by force of it.' For when they see the Cross, they are reminded of the Crucified; they fear Him who has 'smashed the heads of the dragons.' Despise not the seal as a free gift, but rather for this reason honor your Benefactor all the more."[10]

The sign of the cross, made privately at prayer or in the public liturgy of the church, has become omnipresent in Christian life, and as our opening comment from New Testament scholar Donald Senior makes clear, well beyond active Christian living. It is an external sign of Christian communion with Christ. Baptized into Christ we become Body of Christ, and the sign of Christ's self-gift now becomes the sign of our self-giving in his name. The sign of the cross signifies prayer, communion with Christ, and self-giving. It has been nicely expressed by Orthodox theologian Andreas Andreopoulos: "The sign of the cross as a prayer is not a mere request for help and courage for the little personal crosses we may bear in our own life (all told this certainly is one of its obvious messages). The sign of the cross signifies our participation in the body of the church. The sign throughout history has been an

10. Cyril of Jerusalem, *Catechetical Lecture* 13:36. For some background on Cyril, see Young and Teal, *From Nicaea to Chalcedon*, 185–93, and Cummings, *Eucharistic Doctors*, 46–56.

identifying mark of Christianity, its mystical significance connecting each of us with the larger body of the church and with the Crucified Christ."[11] Essentially this is what St. Paul was talking about to the Galatians in the middle of the first century: "I have been crucified with Christ; it is no longer I who live, but Christ lives in me; and the life which I now live in the flesh I live by faith in the Son of God, who loved me and gave himself for me" (Gal 2:20). Christ and the Christian are one-d in communion, and neither may be appropriately thought of without the other; or in the more personal words of Andreopoulos, "When we trace the cross on our body, we actively invite it—we become the cross."[12] Now it is time for us to move on to a consideration of the Stations of the Cross, in which we walk the way of the cross.

11. Andreopoulos, *Sign of the Cross*, 102.
12. Ibid., 10.

2

The Stations of the Cross

Among other devotions, the one that perhaps most vividly encourages and fosters our active sharing in the life and ministry of our Lord is the one known as the Stations of the Cross, or Way of the Cross. In this devotion, we walk with him on the way to Calvary.

—John Macquarrie[1]

There is a kind of tension in Christian faith between the recognition that God is everywhere, nowhere absent, and, therefore, accessible to all wherever they are, and that God became one of us, incarnate in a particular human being, Jesus of Nazareth, at a particular time and in a particular place. Yes, we may find God wherever we happen to be, but Christians have always cherished customs and

1. Macquarrie, *Paths in Spirituality*, 124.

rituals whose very practice invited a closer communion with this ever-present God. One such custom has been the Stations of the Cross, a favorite especially during the holy season of Lent.

There is also a similar kind of tension between the narrative of Christian faith (Scripture, doctrine, worship) and the narrative of personal experience. The Irish novelist and writer Nuala O'Faolain (1940–2008), in her autobiographical memoir, wrote the following about Good Friday, as she wandered into the Pro-Cathedral in Dublin: "[I saw] the purple cloths they cover the images with, during Holy Week, to remind us of Christ's Passion. What about the ordinary passion of people! I thought. Look how much ordinary men and women know about being crucified! No wonder we strain ourselves to believe that there is a God, who loves us."[2] I find that a very sad comment because that is what Good Friday is about, about the crucifixion of ordinary people. Of course, it's about the historic crucifixion that happened once upon a time in Jerusalem. But, since we are conjoined to Christ through baptism, Good Friday is about us joined with Christ, and necessarily so.

The Stations of the Cross are about Christ and us, or perhaps better *us-in-Christ*. That is why we might say that the cross is a school of love. Cardinal Carlo Martini (1927–2012), the great Scripture scholar and former archbishop of Milan, calls the cross a "school of life, a school of humanism." He writes, "Jesus' painful death expects not only our compassion, but our participation. It becomes a *school of life . . . a school of humanism*. We, too, must follow a 'way of the cross' with him if we want to be fully human

2. O'Faolain, *Are You Somebody?*, 198.

and desire life and salvation."[3] If we put these basic ideas about the Stations of the Cross together, then we might say that in the Stations there are three principles for reflection:

- When we speak of our Lord Jesus Christ, we are speaking about a real human being who lived once upon a time, about a man in history. Needless to point out, as we affirm in the Nicene Creed every Sunday our blessed Lord is "consubstantial" with the Father, that is to say, he is divine. Nonetheless, we must not let go of his humanity, every bit as real as ours but without sin.

- Whenever we speak of Jesus Christ, we are also speaking about the church, because there is no Christ without the church. This principle is a reminder to us that the *real Jesus* is not simply the *historical* Jesus. The "historical Jesus" is the one who is studied by historians and biblical scholars of the first century, but the "real Jesus" is so much more. Not only is he risen and ascended and at the Father's right hand, he is also embodied in his Body, the church. To speak of Jesus Christ with any degree of adequacy requires us also to speak of the church.

- Most importantly, therefore, whenever we speak of the church, we are also speaking about ourselves. It is very easy to slip into the bad theological habit of thinking of the "church" as the hierarchy or the ordained. That is simply not the case. The church is all who are baptized into Christ, with the ordained serving this Body of Christ in very particular ways—preaching

3. Martini, *Journeying*, 116. I have rearranged the order but not the meaning of Martini's words here.

the Word, administering the sacraments, leading in mission. The Second Vatican Council, in its Constitution on the Church, says this: "The term laity is here understood to mean all the faithful except those in holy orders and those in a religious state sanctioned by the church. These faithful are by baptism made one body with Christ and are established among the People of God. They are in their own way made sharers in the priestly, prophetic, and kingly functions of Christ. They carry out their own part in the mission of the whole Christian people with respect to the church and the world."[4] Sometimes one gets the impression of the ordained and the laity being pitted against each other rather than working in communion. Sometimes the ordained complain about the laity, and the laity about the ordained. A comment of the German lay Catholic theologian Werner Jeanrond seems very apropos: "Neither clergy nor laity can achieve anything without the other. Hence we must all learn to accept that the Kingdom of God can only be advanced by working together. . . . As so-called lay-Christians we may wish to stop using the excuse of the poor state of the ordained ministry for our own inactivity."[5] Together in communion, not in conflict or competition, ordained and lay must see themselves as the Body of Christ, with different roles and functions, working in mission, in evangelization.

4. Par. 31. See Abbott and Gallagher, *Documents of Vatican II*, 57.

5. Jeanrond, *Call and Response*, 18–20.

The Stations of the Cross

With these fundamental principles in mind, we now proceed to think about the Stations of the Cross. As we do so, we might think of the Stations as having both a historical dimension, reflecting the history of the first Good Friday, and an ecclesial-experiential dimension, reflecting the existential situation and experiences of those who are the Body of Christ. Theologian John Macquarrie emphatically reminds us of the importance of this particular point as we make our way through the Stations of the Cross: "If we are not just spectators gazing curiously at a series of pictures but allowing the scenes to catch us up, as it were, so that we belong in them . . . then we must find ourselves identified with some or other of the personages in these scenes."[6] In other words, as we pray our way through the Stations, Macquarrie tells us that we will find ourselves aligned experientially with some of those portrayed historically in the Stations in one way or another. As we do so, we shall call upon the insights of various theologians and spiritual writers who can help situate us, as it were, in each of the Stations.

STATION 1: JESUS IS CONDEMNED TO DEATH

Historically, this station reminds us that Jesus was betrayed by Judas, and the condemnation then followed under Pontius Pilate. Existentially, this station brings to our minds the betrayals we commit and the condemnations that we issue, as well as the betrayals and condemnations that we experience ourselves. In terms of betrayal, none

6. Macquarrie, *Paths in Spirituality*, 126.

of the apostles, and certainly none of us, has the right to feel superior to Judas. We have all, in one way or another, already betrayed friends. We are Judas.

We are also Pontius Pilate. We are too ready to condemn those who are different from us or who hold different points of view, those who are simply "other" than us. "He is black, and blacks are dangerous. He is gay, and gays are perverts. He is a Jew, and Jews cannot be trusted. He is a refugee, and refugees are threats to our economy. He is an outsider, saying what we do not want to hear, and reminding us of what we would rather forget. He upsets our well-ordered lives."[7] Yet, Dominican theologian Timothy Radcliffe offers us the final, consoling and almost unbelievable thought—that while we betray and condemn others, and through betrayal and condemnation, in a sense, condemn Jesus, he is always forgiving and merciful.[8]

STATION 2: JESUS RECEIVES HIS CROSS

Historically, we face here the *horrendous* nature of crucifixion—its physical reality, its use by the Romans as a deterrent to all troublemakers, and ultimately the humiliation factor. The cross was intended as a public instrument of torture and death that would deter others from any kind of action that would threaten the *Pax Romana*, the fragile peace that governed the Roman Empire. Jesus of Nazareth was seen as a threat to that peace, and so he had to receive the cross.

7. Nouwen, *Walk with Jesus*, 18.
8. Radcliffe, *Stations of the Cross*, 14.

Humankind carries the cross as well. Most ordinary human beings recognize the moral obligation to assist others in carrying their crosses in life. We are moved to try to do something to help. There is also the importance of acknowledging and carrying my own cross, and while assisting others to bear their cross may have its own challenges, trying to face up to my own cross of pain can be even more difficult. Henri Nouwen writes, "The cross of loneliness and isolation, the cross of the rejections I experience, the cross of my depression and inner anguish. As long as I agonize over the pain of others far away but cannot carry the pain that is uniquely mine, I may become an activist, even a defender of humanity, but not yet a follower of Jesus."[9] It is impossible not to hear something of Nouwen's own pain and suffering in life in these words—pain and suffering that have come to light in the biographies that have been written about him.

STATIONS 3, 7, 9: JESUS FALLS BENEATH THE WEIGHT OF THE CROSS

As we attempt with the wealth of historical information now available to reconstruct the last hours of Jesus of Nazareth, it is likely that he would have carried only the crossbeam to his place of execution. The upright part of the cross would have been a permanent fixture. These stations recognize Jesus falling under the weight of that crossbeam. Add to that his experience of being brutally beaten and crowned with thorns, the blood loss, and his rapidly increasing weakness. And, of course, there is the

9. Nouwen, *Walk with Jesus*, 21.

inner psychological violence to contend with, the betrayal by a friend and unjust condemnation to death.

We are constantly falling—physically falling, perhaps, as we age or become ill (and the consequent embarrassment) and, of course, morally falling. All human beings experience moral failure. Especially when preparing to encounter the merciful love of God in the forgiveness of the Sacrament of Penance and Reconciliation, I find myself using those beautiful words of the Anglican mystic-priest-poet George Herbert (1593–1633) in the poem titled "Discipline":

> Though I fail, I weep:
> Though I halt in pace,
> > Yet I creep
> To the throne of grace.[10]

Our falling (failing) should make us weep. Think of the hurt we cause others through our words and actions (not to mention neglecting to speak or act when we should), most especially to those who are close to us. Conjoined to Jesus Christ through baptism-confirmation-Eucharist, and sustained and strengthened in Christ through ongoing reception of the Eucharist, our moral lives seldom match our eucharistic identity. Made Body of Christ, we do not live consistently as Body of Christ.[11] We fail and we fall.

As we know all too well these days, in our world of almost daily news about the sexual and physical abuse of children, about human trafficking, there is another dimension to human falling (failing), and that is children. Children, so innocent and so vulnerable, everywhere and

10. Herbert, *Complete English Poems*, 169.
11. See Cummings, "Sacraments," 246–47.

every day are falling and being felled. This is how Henri Nouwen describes the horror: "All over the world, children fall under the weight of violence, war, corruption, and human anguish. They are hungry, hungry for affection and food. In the cold halls of institutions, they sit . . . waiting for someone to pay attention. They sleep with strangers who use them to satisfy their own desires. They roam the streets of the big cities trying to survive alone or in small bands. There are thousands, yes, millions of them all over the world." And this leads Nouwen to conclude, "Jesus is the innocent child falling under the heavy burden of the cross of human anguish—powerless, weak, and very vulnerable."[12]

STATION 4: JESUS MEETS HIS MOTHER

From the point of view of what actually happened en route to Calvary on that first Good Friday, we do not know if Jesus actually met his mother. And yet, one has to ask: Could Mary have stayed away from what she knew was going on? It seems impossible that she was not there among the crowd, watching and wondering, her heart breaking. What must she have felt while watching him bleed and stumble toward his death?

It is a terrible thing to watch your child die, the most terrible thing ever. "The death of a child before his or her parents is outrageous. It contradicts the natural order of things. It is the child who ought to care for parents and bury them."[13] That has never happened to me, but it happened

---

12. Nouwen, *Walk with Jesus*, 32.
13. Radcliffe, *Stations of the Cross*, 27.

to one of my dearest friends, Seymour, and his wife, Paula. Their son, Amos, had a virulent form of leukemia. They sat by Amos's bed many a day and night. When the doctors told them, as Amos slipped into unconsciousness, that there was nothing more they could do, they watched their little son quietly die in front of them. Seymour and Paula took Amos home for the last time, telling him how much they loved him, all that he had meant to them in his too short thirteen years. Next day, Seymour went to the store, bought some walnut wood, made the casket for his son, and laid him to rest in it. The cross that hangs over my desk was made by Seymour from the shavings of Amos's casket.

STATION 5: SIMON OF CYRENE HELPS JESUS CARRY HIS CROSS

We know from the gospel narrative (Matt 27:32; Mark 15:21; Luke 23:26) that this man Simon, from North Africa (modern Libya), was pressed into helping Jesus carry the cross. Mark notes that he was the father of two well-known Christians, Alexander and Rufus. Jesus needed Simon to help him carry his cross, and it may be that through helping to carry the cross of Jesus he came to be a disciple.

"In Jesus, we see God needing us."[14] It can sound strange to Western theological ears to speak of God needing us, needing anything, so accustomed are we to thinking of God as having no needs whatever. Perhaps this particular station is telling us that having "needs" is not necessarily a deficit, but an invitation to let others reach out to us, even as we reach out to them in their need. Jesus needs us to

14. Ibid., 30.

help others carry crosses, or, better, to help him in others' carrying the cross, and like Jesus we also need help. I love these words of Henri Nouwen: "Jesus needs us to fulfil his mission. He needs people to carry the cross with him and for him. . . . The hard, painful work of salvation is a work in which God becomes dependent upon human beings. Yes, God is full of power, glory, and majesty. But God chose to be among us as one of us—as a dependent human being. . . . Every time I am willing to break out of my false need for self-sufficiency and dare to ask for help, a new community emerges—a fellowship of the weak—strong in the trust that together we can be a people of hope for a broken world. Simon of Cyrene discovered a new communion."[15]

STATION 6: VERONICA WIPES THE FACE OF JESUS

It is generally recognized that this station is the stuff of Christian imagination. The scholars tell us that there was no historical Veronica on this walk to Calvary. No such person is mentioned in any of the four gospels. Yet that it is imaginary does not mean that it lacks truthful insight. The truth of the matter is that we are all called to be Veronica. Veronica's name means "true icon, true likeness." In reaching out to Jesus, she helped him. As Jesus was Love fleshed for others, so Veronica was love fleshed for him. Like the imaginary Veronica, we are to flesh love to others and become his true likeness. We are all called to be the true icon or likeness of Jesus. As Timothy Radcliffe notes, "It belongs

---

15. Nouwen, *Walk with Jesus*, 35.

to the ministry of every baptized person to be the face of Christ in the ordinary interactions of our daily lives."[16]

In his marvelous novel *Monsignor Quixote*, Graham Greene describes with gentleness and humor the growing love that develops between Don Quixote, parish priest in a Spanish village, and Enrique Zancas, the communist mayor of the same village. They set out on a great adventure together like Don Quixote and Sancho Panza of Cervantes' fame.[17] In the course of the novel, Don Quixote thinks of the human face as "the mirror image of God."[18] As we look into a human face, we are looking at the mirror image of the God who is faceless but who becomes face-d in others. Think on these challenging words of Caryll Houselander: "In Christ burying his face in that woman's veil . . . we see grown-up people who have been maimed or disfigured, those whom chronic illness or infirmity has embittered. . . . We see those most tragic ones among old people, those who are not loved and are not wanted by their own, those in whom the ugliness, not the beauty of old age is visible. We see the tragic ones who are all but cut off from the very few by mental illness."[19] Veronica's station may be imaginative not historical, but who could deny its truth?

16. Radcliffe, *Stations of the Cross*, 35.

17. See Cummings, "Greene and Quixote's Final Eucharist," 124–31, and also "Grace of Graham Greene," 65–76.

18. Greene, *Monsignor Quixote*, 115. I owe this reference to Radcliffe, *Stations of the Cross*, 34, 70.

19. Houselander, *Way of the Cross*, 68.

STATION 7: JESUS SPEAKS TO THE WOMEN OF JERUSALEM

It seems to have been the case that when Jews were crucified by the Romans—and that was often—the women of Jerusalem would gather to lament the death. They would weep and mourn for the one executed. This is what they do for Jesus the Jew. There is no human being who does not understand the reality of tears.

Our Christian spiritual tradition speaks of the gift of years, the gift of weeping. We all know how comforting it can be when someone weeps in solidarity with us, and how healing it can be when we weep for what we've done, or when we weep for another. In 1623, the English priest-poet John Donne preached a sermon on that sad verse in St. John's Gospel, "Jesus wept." The Lord had wept at the death of his friend Lazarus, and Donne sets out to understand what that means. Tears and weeping are important to God, he believes, because God sees our tears and hears our weeping. God can work with those who can weep. They have hearts of flesh, not of stone. But then Donne turns his attention to people who cannot or will not weep, and he says this: "When God shall come to that last act in the glorifying of man, when he promises, *to wipe all tears from his eyes*, what shall God have to do with that eye that never wept?"[20] Donne suggests that the one who cannot weep has put himself beyond God's help. Do I know how to weep?

20. Sermon XIII, "Compassion of Christ," in *Sermons of John Donne*, 331.

STATION 10: JESUS IS STRIPPED
OF HIS GARMENTS

Those who were about to be executed by crucifixion by the Romans were stripped naked so as to complete their utter humiliation and degradation. Being stripped naked was especially degrading for a Jew, whose religion cultivated modesty. One can imagine how Jesus must have felt.

Again turning to the ever-insightful Henri Nouwen for existential commentary on this station of the stripping of Jesus's garments, we read: "All human dignity is gone. . . . Countless are the old men and women who live their stripped down existences hidden away from the fast-moving world of our century. Their growing old has left them with nothing but their naked existence, completely dependent upon the randomly bestowed favors or rejections of their milieu. The stripped body of Jesus reveals to us the immense degradation that human beings suffer all through the world, at all places and in all times."[21]

STATION 11: JESUS IS NAILED TO
THE CROSS

No gospel account of the crucifixion of Jesus actually tells us whether Jesus was nailed to the cross or tied to the cross. Scripture scholar Raymond Brown says that nailing to the cross is implied in scenes after the death of Jesus—for example, in Luke 24:39, where Jesus says to the apostles, "Look at my hands and my feet," and in John 20:25, where Thomas says, "Unless I see the marks of the nails in his

---

21. Nouwen, *Walk with Jesus*, 47.

hands . . ."[22] Whatever about the exact historical circumstances lying behind the pericope about Thomas placing his fingers in Jesus's wounds, Christian devotion and art have emphasized Jesus being nailed to the cross.

In his beautiful commentary Timothy Radcliffe writes of this station, "He was nailed to the cross, nailed firmly to all our failures, identified with everyone who seems to be a letdown, the child who disappoints a parent, the husband or wife who turned out to have feet of clay, the disgraced priest. He embraces all those who feel that God has abandoned them. . . . In him, no life is a dead end."[23] I notice several things about Radcliffe's words here. Radcliffe uses the passive voice. Jesus is necessarily the recipient of all that is done to him, and in that sense he is passive. I don't suppose that he could have done anything at this point but let it happen. Resistance was not only futile, it was impossible. For one who is afraid of all kinds of needles, the pain of having one's wrists and feet nailed to the cross is unimaginable. Perhaps one wishes for it all to be over. At the same time, and especially in the Gospel of St. John, one has the sense of Jesus not as a hapless victim before the brutality of the Romans, but as one who in regal style is in control of the situation and so embraces the cross. As we read the gospels, his constant interiority seems to have been to let the awful things that we humans do to one another be done to him. He does not anticipate and so evade betrayal by Judas and being handed over to the authorities. He lets betrayal happen. He makes no attempt to contest the done deals of his unjust trials. He lets them happen. Now he lets the nailing to the cross happen,

22. Brown, *Death of the Messiah*, 2:949.
23. Radcliffe, *Stations of the Cross*, 54.

tasting to the end the toxicity with which we humans afflict one another. It is an active passivity, because in this seeming passivity Jesus shows the extent of God's love for his human creatures. He wants to taste the totality of what is so often our wretched human condition. God submits: "He embraces all those who feel that God has abandoned them, and no life is a dead end."

STATION 12: JESUS DIES ON THE CROSS

At the time of Jesus, crucifixion was a Roman form of extreme punishment, especially for slaves and revolutionaries of any sort.[24] Used mainly for its deterrence value, it could not be the mode of execution for a Roman citizen. That is why in the tradition St. Peter was crucified, while St. Paul, a Roman citizen, was beheaded. Beheading was swift; crucifixion could last for days. In his greatly weakened condition, Jesus's death took only a few hours.

What was going through Jesus's mind during these last hours? The meditations later in the book on the "Seven Last Words of Jesus" will offer some material for reflection. At this point, let's just stay with the fact of Jesus's death. That fact is virtually impenetrable to us, for a number of reasons. This is what Timothy Radcliffe writes: "What can we say of anyone's death, since we do not know what it is to be dead? Dying we know, but not death. What possible words can we have for the death of God? The Word of God is silenced. What words do we have? Yet this dead man on the cross is the Word that speaks most loudly of

24. Harrington, *Jesus*, 70.

a love beyond imagination."[25] Death is of its very nature impenetrable. The twentieth-century philosopher Jean-Paul Sartre famously said that death "removes all meaning from life."[26] Sartre is surely correct in pointing to what I am calling the impenetrability of death. But from our Christian standpoint, if the Eternal Word of God made flesh in Jesus has tasted this reality of death, then it is not entirely impenetrable. God has been there. God knows what death is like from the inside, as it were. That conviction does not remove the sadness from death. The sadness of death is the price we pay for loving another. The eternal life of Love that is the communion of the Trinity, however, is the final word on the matter for Christians. We believe that our end is to be taken up into that Communion of Love. And, as Radcliffe has said, that Love is "beyond imagination."

STATION 13: JESUS IS TAKEN DOWN FROM THE CROSS

Normally in this penultimate station we remember not simply the taking down of Jesus's dead body from the cross but also his body being laid in the arms of his mother, Mary. There is not much to be said about his being taken down from the cross. If we follow the narrative sequence of St. John's Gospel, we are given some sense of urgency about this. "Since it was the day of Preparation, the Jews did not want the bodies left on the cross during the sabbath, especially because that sabbath was a day of great solemnity.

---

25. Radcliffe, *Seven Last Words*, 57.
26. Sartre, *Being and Nothingness*, 539.

So they asked Pilate to have the legs of the crucified men broken and the bodies removed" (John 19:31).

The narrative tells us nothing about Jesus's corpse being placed in the arms of his mother. Natural human affection and Christian piety and devotion provide what is missing textually from the story. She was there and she held him. The assumption is made that our Lady Mary was widowed at this time, especially since there is no mention whatever of Joseph during the ministry of Jesus. One can imagine something of the thoughts of a widowed mother on this occasion: Why did it all have to come to this? Where did we go wrong? How am I to come to terms with the death of my child? Yet again I find myself profoundly moved by the words of Timothy Radcliffe: "Mary holds her dead child tenderly. He is past feeling but this tenderness is right. It is his body. We are gentle with the bodies of those whom we love." One can feel the sadness behind these words. Radcliffe, however, excellent theologian that he is, will not allow us to stay there in our sadness. He goes on to proclaim, "We must not wait to show our gentleness until someone is dead. Be tender while it can be felt and reciprocated. Say the word of love or gratitude while it can be heard."[27] Nothing more needs to be said, but much needs to be done.

STATION 14: JESUS IS LAID
IN THE TOMB

Let's think about the burial of Jesus in the Gospel of St. Matthew 27:57–61. "When it was evening, there came a

27. Radcliffe, *Seven Last Words*, 2.

rich man from Arimathea, named Joseph, who was also a disciple of Jesus. He went to Pilate and asked for the body of Jesus; then Pilate ordered it to be given to him. So Joseph took the body and wrapped it in a clean linen cloth and laid it in his own new tomb, which he had hewn in the rock. He then rolled a great stone to the door of the tomb and went away. Mary Magdalene and the other Mary were there, sitting opposite the tomb." Matthew informs us that Joseph was a disciple of Jesus; a more accurate translation of the Greek might be "he was discipled" to or by Jesus. This verb is also used in 28:19 when the eleven are commissioned by Jesus to "make disciples of all nations." It may at first sight seem strange that Pilate acquiesces in Joseph's request for the body of Jesus, who, after all, was executed as a criminal. Recalling, however, that in Matthew's Gospel and only there Pilate was told by his wife that Jesus was a just man and that he had publicly washed his hands to underscore Jesus's innocence, he may have been disposed to grant Joseph's request. All the way through the narrative of the passion and death, Jesus has been handed over from one hostile agent to another. "Now finally he is not given over again but given back to one who loves him."[28]

Visiting the graves of those whom we love can assist our human grieving as well as provide hope. Perhaps that was what Mary Magdalene and the other Mary were doing. They were witnesses to the death of Jesus, and now at his burial place they mourn his passing on Good Friday. On Easter Day, Mary Magdalene and the other Mary return to the tomb to continue their mourning (Matt 28:1), and their hope is strengthened by the appearance and message

28. Brown, *Death of the Messiah*, 2:1226.

of the angel of the resurrection: "Do not be afraid; I know that you are looking for Jesus who was crucified. He is not here; for he has been raised, as he said. Come, see the place where he lay" (Matt 28:5–6). In all probability the "other Mary" is Mary the mother of Jesus.[29] Along with Joseph of Arimathea, the two Marys form a community of love and hope around Jesus.

CONCLUSION

The best way to conclude this chapter on the Stations of the Cross is with some wonderful words of the little-known Capuchin friar Benedict Canfield (1563–1611). Benedict was the religious name of William Fitch of Little Canfield, Essex. Benedict became a Catholic and a Capuchin; he studied at Douai and Paris. He is the author of several works, the best known of which is his *Rule of Perfection*, published in 1609. In this little book we find this remarkable passage: "Therefore our own pains—insofar as they are not ours but those of Christ—must be deeply respected. How wonderful! And more: our pains are as much to be revered as those of Jesus Christ in His own passion. For if people correctly adore Him with so much devotion in images on the Good Friday cross, why may we not then revere Him on the living cross that we ourselves are?" That last sentence of Benedict's, "Why may we not then revere Him on the living cross that we ourselves are?" is an apt summary of the reflections shared in the first two chapters of this book. It is in that same spirit of mystical communion with Christ that we move on to meditate on the seven last words of Jesus from the cross.

29. See, among others, Hare, *Matthew*, 330.

3

The First Word from the Cross

"Father, forgive them; they know not what they do."

The first word is taken from the Gospel according to Luke (23:33–34).

When they came to the place called the Skull, they crucified him and the criminals there, one on his right, the other on his left. Then Jesus said, "Father, forgive them, they know not what they do."

The last words of a person are especially significant. I have never actually heard a dying person's final words. In my experience, often the dying slip out of this world unconscious, with nothing to say. To hear someone's final, conscious words is a great privilege indeed. On the brink of that moment of death, words take on a special significance and meaning.

The Dying of Jesus

We do not know the exact words of the dying Jesus on the cross. No one was there with a sheet of papyrus or a stylus and tablet to take them down for posterity. What we have in the gospel narratives of Jesus's dying and death are pastoral-theological meditations that served ancient Christians well not only when they thought of Jesus's dying and death but also when they faced their own dying and death. Our service on this Good Friday helps us think about the last words of Jesus as they are represented in the gospels, and helps us make these words our own.

"Father, forgive them, they know not what they do." These words of Jesus from St. Luke's Gospel must have been a major factor leading to Dante's judgment that St. Luke is "the scribe of the gentleness of Christ."[1] Here is Jesus, writhing in agony, on the point of death, and he speaks of forgiveness for those who have put him on this cross. Forgiveness of others is a constant theme in the Gospel of St. Luke, "especially from a Jesus who teaches his disciples to love their enemies."[2] "Love your enemies, do good to those who hate you, bless those who curse you, pray for those who abuse you" (Luke 6:27–28). The Jesus of Luke's Gospel sketches a picture of God as always generous in offering forgiveness.

This is the God imaged as the father in the parable of the Prodigal Son: "So he went off and went to his father. But while he was still far off, his father saw him and was filled with compassion; he ran and put his arms around him and kissed him" (Luke 15:20). You will recall from the parable that the prodigal son did not have the best of motives for returning to his father. He was hungry! But that

1. Cited in Brown, *Death of the Messiah*, 2:980.
2. Senior, *Jesus in the Gospel of Luke*, 129.

did not matter for the father. He was watching and waiting, to love and forgive.

This same sentiment of forgiveness is found in St. Ignatius of Antioch, early in the second century, for Christians facing persecution: "Be yourselves *gentle* in answer to their wrath; be humble minded in answer to their proud speaking; offer prayer for their blasphemy; be steadfast in the faith for their error; be *gentle* for their cruelty, and do not seek to retaliate. Let us be proved their brothers by our *gentleness* and let us be imitators of the Lord."[3] One commentator on Ignatius writes of our passage, "Ignatius carefully delineates the Christian attitude of gentleness in a rhetorically constructed series of parallel clauses on a free tradition of the words of Jesus,"[4] and he points to the Lord's words in Matt 5:39–42: "But I say to you, Do not resist an evildoer. But if anyone strikes you on the right cheek, turn the other also; and if anyone wants to sue you and take your coat, give your cloak as well; and if anyone forces you to go one mile, go also the second mile. Give to everyone who begs from you, and do not refuse anyone who wants to borrow from you." If these words of Jesus and Ignatius speak anything to our hearts, they speak gentleness. If we scroll back to the Beatitudes in the same Sermon on the Mount we come to Matt 5:5, "Blessed are the *gentle*, for they will inherit the earth." The NRSV reads "meek" here, but the Greek word is *praus*, "gentle," and this is the word Ignatius uses. It is also the word Jesus uses of himself: "Take my yoke upon you and learn from me; for I am

---

3. Ignatius, *To the Ephesians* 10:2–3, in Lake, *Apostolic Fathers*, 1:185.

4. Schoedel, *Ignatius of Antioch*, 69.

gentle and humble in heart, and you will find rest for your souls" (Matt 11:29).

"Gentle" is such a lovely word. The emphasis of St. Ignatius on gentleness reminds me of one of my grandchildren, Cora. She is two years old. In her daycare center, whenever there is any disagreement over a toy or something like that, and an inclination to take the toy or to push the one who has it, the caregivers counsel, "Soft hands, gentle hands." Jesus must have had soft hands, gentle hands.

Who were they who needed this forgiveness, the gentle hands offered by Jesus? The Romans who carried out the execution, the Jewish leaders who sought it, assuredly. Perhaps more than anyone, the Romans and the Jewish leaders needed the forgiveness of Jesus. But it is surely interesting that this passage about forgiveness is missing from a number of very early manuscripts of St. Luke's Gospel. One wonders why. Was this passage about forgiveness there in the original autograph manuscript but omitted by later copyists of the Gospel? That seems to have been the case. Later copyists left out this final word of Jesus on the cross about forgiveness.[5] You might wonder what possible reason there could be for a scribe to omit what has been described as "the most beautiful sentence in the passion narrative." The answer, sadly, seems to be that "there would have been few second-century copyists anxious to have Jesus pray for forgiveness for the Jews."[6] The copyists did not want the dying Jesus to be heard offering forgiveness to the Jews, and so they quite deliberately left these words out. What an enormously tragic omission! No gentle hands for the Jews.

5. Brown, *Death of the Messiah*, 2:980.
6. Ibid.

In the same tragic vein, St. John Chrysostom could write the very opposite of this prayer of Jesus in respect of the Jews. "After you killed Christ . . . There is no hope left for you, no rectification, no excuse."[7] This is hardly in line with the sentiments of Jesus. How easy it is for us Christians to corrupt the message of Jesus, the message of forgiveness, and establish categories of those who are worthy and those who are unworthy of God's forgiveness.

Ultimately, however, we are all implicated in this execution and so we are all blessed in this forgiveness of Jesus. As a rabbi of the twentieth century, Abraham Joshua Heschel, put it, "Some are guilty, all are responsible."[8] The authorities who condemned Jesus are guilty. Rabbi Heschel suggests that we are all implicated in contributing to what we might call "the sin of the world," the history of accumulated wrongdoing for which each one of us is responsible. "Each" is much too abstract here. It's not "each," it is me and it is you. If I protest that I have never done anything egregiously bad, that I am really not such a skilled sinner, then I am a liar, or a fool, or both. It is the wrong that I do in the bad habits of every day, "the everyday forms of the habits of compromise, of loves betrayed, of lies excused, of dreams deferred until they die."[9] Again, this is much too abstract. *I* have compromised, *I* have lied, *I* have betrayed love, *I* have let dreams die.

We are too often petty and pusillanimous. Not so Jesus of Nazareth. He died as he lived, absolutely generous and magnanimous, calling God his Abba/Father in

7. Chrysostom, *Adversus Judaeos Oratio* 6:2 (PG 48:907), cited in ibid.

8. Cited in Neuhaus, *Death on a Friday Afternoon*, 19.

9. Ibid., 15.

our passage, and praying this final message of forgiveness. "Father, forgive them, they know not what they do." In offering the gentle hands of forgiveness in these his very last moments of life, he reveals to us that our God is nothing but Love, and Love always forgives. In the words of the nineteenth-century Scottish Presbyterian minister and hymn-writer George Matheson (1842–1906), God is the love that will not let us go. Here are the words of the first stanza of Matheson's hymn with that title:

> O Love that wilt not let me go,
> I rest my weary soul in thee;
> I give thee back the life I owe,
> That in thine ocean depths its flow
> May richer, fuller be.

4

The Second Word from the Cross

"Today you will be with me in Paradise."

The second word is taken from the Gospel according to Luke (23:39–42).

Now one of the criminals hanging there reviled Jesus, saying, "Are you not the Messiah? Save yourself and us." The other, however, rebuking him, said in reply, "Have you no fear of God, for you are subject to the same condemnation? And indeed, we have been condemned justly, for the sentence we received corresponds to our crimes, but this man had done nothing criminal." Then he said, "Jesus, remember me when you come into your kingdom." He replied to him, "Amen, I say to you, today you will be with me in Paradise."

Perhaps it is not all that important, but the traditional word "thief" as in "good thief" does not occur in this text. Instead the word is *kakourgos*, the Greek for "wrongdoer." This anonymous "wrongdoer" was crucified alongside Jesus in the narrative. Let's stay, however, with the traditional translation, "the good thief." Timothy Radcliffe has it right when he describes this wrongdoer in the customary way as "the good thief." Why? Radcliffe writes, "It is a good description. [The good thief] knows how to get hold of what is not his. He pulls off the most amazing coup in history. He gets paradise without paying for it. As do we all. We just have to learn how to accept gifts."[1]

New Testament scholars speculate that this story about the good thief may very well be a Lucan theological creation, coming from St. Luke's creative theological genius.[2] St. Luke was a masterly, creative storyteller. Think of the parable of the Good Samaritan or the parable of the Prodigal Son, both parables found only in St. Luke's Gospel. Think of the stunning theological reality of the Infancy Gospel in Luke 1–2, and the stories of the Annunciation and the Visitation. At the end of the day, there really is no way to know whether these particular final words of the dying Jesus were actually spoken by him or not. Whether it is Luke's creation or not, the text continues the theme of forgiveness already noted in the "First Word" as prominent in the Gospel of St. Luke.

Think back for a moment to the parable of the Prodigal Son in Luke 15. Forgiveness is given to the son by his father even before the young man has had an opportunity to say that he is sorry: "I have sinned against heaven

1. Radcliffe, *Seven Last Words*, 26.
2. Brown, *Death of the Messiah*, 2:1001.

and before you" (Luke 15:21). The father simply forgives, throwing his arms around his contrite son and welcoming him home. The father in the parable is himself a parable of God the Father. He forgives and offers healing. God is invisible, but becomes uniquely manifest in Jesus, and Jesus consistently forgives and offers healing. Just a few verses earlier in St. Luke's passion narrative we read about Jesus healing at the time of his arrest, and, even earlier, becoming as it were the agent of healing between King Herod and the Roman procurator Pontius Pilate. "The Lucan Jesus healed the ear of the high priest's servant who was hostile to him. His very presence healed the enmity that had existed between Herod and Pilate. He spontaneously pleaded with his Father for forgiveness for those who crucified him."[3] And now, with soft and gentle hands, he addresses this thief.

Notice how the good thief addresses Jesus. Details in the Gospel narrative are always interesting and are so seldom noticed. The thief addresses Jesus simply as "Jesus." That may not strike one as especially significant until one realizes that no one else in the Gospel addresses Jesus directly by his name without some qualification such as "Lord" or "Master." Addressing Jesus by name is "stunning in its intimacy. . . . The first person with the confidence to be so familiar is a convicted criminal who is also the last person on earth to speak to Jesus before Jesus dies."[4] If Love is the logic of the universe, then words of intimacy, words of love are the words that really count in the end. Few things are more intimate than addressing someone

3. Ibid., 1005. Luke 23:12 reads, "That same day Herod and Pilate became friends with each other; before this they had been enemies."

4. Ibid.

by name, especially their first name. It may be in part a cultural thing, but when I am addressed as "Cummings," I feel somewhat objectified and alienated. Addressed as "Owen," I am at ease and open up to the one speaking to me. In the gospels, think of Mary of Magdala weeping in grief and mourning at the tomb of Jesus. The tomb is empty. She thinks the body of Jesus has been taken away. She thinks he is the gardener. She does not know what to make of the resurrection until Jesus addresses her by name, "Mary" (John 20:16). Addressed by name, the meaning of the resurrection begins to unfold and Mary brings the good news to the apostles. She becomes the "apostle of the apostles."

Although Jesus does not speak the good thief's name, he speaks to him intimately. The good thief asked to be remembered by Jesus: "Jesus, remember me when you come into your kingdom." The intimacy emerges in Jesus's promise to him: "Amen, I say to you, today you will be with me in paradise." The good thief has become a disciple. He wants to be remembered by Jesus. This request to be remembered is by implication a desire to be a disciple of Jesus. Further, he becomes a disciple who is promised paradise with Jesus, "the highest heaven for final bliss in God's presence."[5]

To be is to be presenced in God. As human beings we are always presenced in God. God is never absent. God is the one in whom we live, and move, and have our being. "Paradise" is the final fullness of this being presenced in God that is already ours. However, we are not always present to the God who is never absent from us. It is a lifelong process of invitation and response. We need

5. Ibid., 1010–11.

to consent daily to this conviction and let it saturate our consciousness. "God says to each of us, 'It is wonderful that you exist.'"[6] That's just it. God takes delight in us, not just us generically, so to speak, as part of the human tribe, but in each of us individually. God loves us, not just as an impersonal number in an anonymous global crowd, but each one of us personally. One author has put it like this: "There is nothing very astonishing about a God who loves us relentlessly, except that we generally do not believe in one."[7] It's really hard to believe in a God like that because it's impossible for us to love like that. God desires, loves, and forgives us with such astonishing generosity that we find it very hard to imagine and take seriously.[8]

Really, the only thing to say to this Lovely God every day and often is, "Thank you." Abbot Peter McCarthy, OCSO, of the Trappist Abbey in Oregon, in his funeral homily for a senior member of the community, Fr. Dismas, who was struggling through the last stages of cancer, describes Fr. Dismas's final words to his Trappist brothers: "He was continually saying 'thank you' to health care workers, to hospice staff, to visiting friends and finally the last words to his brothers gathered around his bed in the infirmary. . . . [I said to him], 'Father, would you like to say a few words to the community?' [He replied], 'No. Just thank you, thank you, everyone.'"[9] Fr. Dismas's constant words as he neared the end were simply, "Thank you." No comment is needed to clarify his meaning. The simple

6. Radcliffe, *Seven Last Words*, 28.

7. Burtchaell, *Philemon's Problem*, 42.

8. See Ford, *Shape of Living*, 38.

9. Abbot Peter McCarthy, OCSO, funeral homily for Fr. Dismas, March 13, 2012; quoted with permission.

recognition that everything and everyone is gift from God called forth "thank you, everyone." Although it's not in the gospel narrative, tradition has it that the name of the good thief was Dismas. Jesus said to Dismas on the cross, "Today you will be with me in Paradise." Jesus, hopefully, will say that to us one day too. And our response, hopefully, will be that of the latter-day Trappist Dismas: "Thank you."

5

The Third Word from the Cross

"Woman, behold your son . . . behold your mother."

The third word is taken from the Gospel according to John (19:25–27).

Standing by the cross of Jesus were his mother and his mother's sister, Mary the wife of Clopas, and Mary of Magdala. When Jesus saw his mother and the disciple there whom he loved, he said to his mother, "Woman, behold your son." Then he said to the disciple, "Behold your mother." And from that hour the disciple took her into his home.

One woman has written about Calvary, "As a mother, I cannot imagine Mary's suffering at the foot of the cross. It is for those women who have been in that desolate place, in the Golgotha that has had too many names in our

bloody human history, to grope their way toward articulat-
ing their experience. Ultimately, the mother at the foot of
her child's cross occupies a space beyond language.... We
struggle toward meaning."[1] It's true. How could you know
what's going on in the heart of Jesus's mother as she watches
the child she carried for nine months in her womb bleed to
death? We do no honor to Our Lady if we think of her possessing a detailed knowledge of what Jesus was about, or
the Resurrection to come. She must have been devastated
as she watched her son crumbling, bleeding to death; and
without Joseph by her side, she may have thought, "Where
did we go wrong? How has it all come to this?" The only
ones who can comment are those who have witnessed the
bloody deaths of their own sons and daughters: on 9/11,
in Iraq or Afghanistan, on the streets of our cities, in our
cancer hospitals.

This scene at Calvary is a "puzzling scene."[2] What is
so puzzling? For a start, we don't really know for sure who
was standing close to Jesus on the cross. The gospels provide us with different names and different persons. Mark,
the earliest Gospel, says there were many women "looking
on from afar, among whom were Mary Magdalene, and
Mary the mother of James the younger and of Joses, and
Salome . . . and also many other women who came up with
him to Jerusalem" (Mark 15:40–41). Matthew, who comes
next chronologically, also tells us that there were many
women; he names Mary Magdalene, and Mary the mother
of James and Joseph, and the mother of the sons of Zebe-
dee (Matt 27:55–56). Luke does not offer us any names,
but simply says that "all his acquaintances and the women

1. Beattie, *Rediscovering Mary*, 111.
2. The phrase is from Gaventa, *Mary*, 89.

from Galilee stood at a distance" (Luke 23:49). And finally, we have this gem of a passage from John. Women are present on Calvary in all the gospels, but John is the only one who mentions a male disciple being there, "the beloved disciple." That description is a little puzzling too.

Good Friday has seen the almost complete disintegration of Jesus's own community. The inner circle of that community has been the Twelve, all called by Jesus to discipleship. Peter always heads the list of the Twelve, and Judas comes last (Mark 3:16–19; Matt 10:2–4; Luke 6:13–16). The list itself is very interesting; it seems to me not merely a chronological list, telling us who was called first by the Lord and who was called last, but a "theological" list. Peter, the first named, will deny Jesus three times, and Judas, the last named, will betray him. In between Peter and Judas we find the others, including James and John, the so-called sons of thunder. After Jesus had told the Twelve for the third time that the Son of Man was going to suffer and die, both James and John, as if they had never ever heard this, request places of privilege—to sit at his right hand and his left hand "in his glory" (Mark 10:37). The list of the Twelve with the little we know about them offers us hints and shades of ourselves. Like them, we have been called by Jesus: "Follow me." And like them, in our following we sometimes get it right and other times wrong. *We* are the Twelve in so many ways, called to follow, to be disciples, and so very predictably we mess up: we deny, we are selfishly ambitious at times, we betray.

The Twelve are nowhere named as present at the cross. Jesus's community of the apostles is absent. Yet in this precious scene from St. John's Gospel we witness a new community coming into being—the community of the church. At the final moment, the moment of dying, we see this new community being born. Death and birth, the rhythm of our evolving universe, the Paschal Mystery. The mother of Jesus is given a son, and the beloved disciple is given a mother.[3]

I mentioned earlier that details in the gospel narrative are always interesting, and in this particular scene, puzzling. Notice that Mary is never called Mary in the Gospel of St. John. And here she is simply called "woman." This seems very puzzling and strange to us—"woman"! It seems so cold and so distant. But there is a reason for her being addressed in this way: she is the new Eve. In the story of creation in the book of Genesis, "the woman"—or as we say, Eve—is the mother of all the living (Gen 3:20). From the earliest Christian times, Mary has been understood as the new Eve. As Eve was the mother of the human family, so the new Eve is the mother of the new Christian family, the church.[4]

Another puzzle: our translation reads "from that hour the disciple took her into his home." It could mean that in a quite literal sense according to the Greek text. That Jesus might have been thinking of his mother and her needs is undoubtedly true, even obvious. Any son on his deathbed would consider the needs of his mother. But St. John in his Gospel *never* writes obviously. Words, phrases, and events have layers of meaning attached to them, and seldom an obvious meaning. Symbol layered upon symbol is the way of St. John. It is as if he is luring us through the multilayered meaning of his words ever more deeply into the mystery of Jesus. That the beloved disciple is just taking

3. Radcliffe, *Seven Last Words*, 33.
4. Brown, *Death of the Messiah*, 2:1021–22.

Mary home is too simplistic and obvious for John. There has to be more to it than that. The fact that the mother of Jesus is now the disciple's mother and that he has taken her "into his own" is deeply symbolic. Mary, who is Jesus's natural birth mother, part of his natural family, now becomes his ecclesial mother, his church-mother, part of his church family, the community of disciples.[5] Now we're getting somewhere. Now we're cracking open something of St. John's less than obvious meaning.

What is that meaning? Here at the foot of the cross we see our church-mother, Mary, and we see ourselves. Each one of us is the beloved disciple. Another detail you may not have noticed is that the beloved disciple is never named in the Gospel of St. John. The only one who is named as being "beloved" by Jesus is Lazarus: the "beloved disciple" is quite literally and deliberately anonymous, and his name is "you" and "me." You and I are the beloved disciple to whom is given a new mother, Mary. St. John's vision is so uniquely his. Shortly after this, we are told by St. John, Jesus "bowed his head and handed over his spirit" (John 19:30). It is as if Good Friday and Pentecost happen on the same day: the death of Jesus, loving us to the end, and the new birth of Jesus that continues his loving in his organic, living body, the church. We might put it like this. As Jesus expired, "handing over his spirit," he inspired the church; he breathed his Spirit into the church. The new family of church breathes with his holy breath. This is the church born from the cross. This is how one theologian sums it up: "In the moment of death, the motherly Kingdom is born. The Mother of God becomes mother of the . . . devastated

5. Ibid., 1024.

community that is represented at the cross by a group of women and one unnamed disciple."[6] This theologian continues in a very contemporary way: "The only male disciple able to expose himself to the experience of the cross is not named. While women become real presences, known by name, the unnamed man becomes a symbol of all men who must learn to live within a motherly church, taking Mary as their example and restoring women to their rightful place."[7] We talk about Mother Mary, and we talk about Mother Church. Much food for thought here . . .

Some years ago, I came across a book entitled *Missing Mary*.[8] Among many other things the author gives a personal account of her "missing Mary" in the post-Vatican II church—the devotions to Mary, Marian processions, etc. While I can understand the sense of loss here, I am unable entirely to identify with it. Mary isn't missing because she is very present in the church, that is to say, among ourselves. The Second Vatican Council placed its treatment of Mary in the final chapter to the Constitution on the Church. Mary becomes a type of the church and first among the community of disciples, following the lead of this scene from St. John's Gospel. She sits with the church. In St. Mary's Catholic Church in Boise, Mary quite literally sits with the church. There is a beautiful carved image of Mary, sitting down in the front pew, sitting with her family as first among the community of disciples. How beautifully appropriate! Mary sits in the front, with the rest of her eucharistic family literally around her. This word of Jesus

6. Beattie, *Rediscovering Mary*, 113.

7. Ibid., 113–14.

8. Spretnak, *Missing Mary*.

from the cross in St. John's Gospel invites us to "take Mary into our own home," eucharistically, as beloved disciples. "Woman, behold your son; son, behold your mother."

6

The Fourth Word from the Cross

"My God, my God, why have you forsaken me?"

The fourth word is taken from the Gospel according to Mark (15:34).

From noon onward, darkness came over the whole land until three in the afternoon. And about three o'clock Jesus cried out in a loud voice, "Eli, Eli, lema sabachthani?" which means, "My God, my God, why have you forsaken me?"

The death of Jesus in St. Mark's Gospel has been described as "the boldest and most challenging among the four evangelists."[1] These words of Jesus, "My God, my God, why have you forsaken me?" are full of darkness; and darkness, we are told, came over the whole land for three

1. Senior, *Jesus in the Gospel of Mark*, 121.

hours immediately before the death of Jesus, so that we are led up to the death of Jesus "through a foreboding tunnel of gloom."[2] It is the gloom of indescribable human suffering. Methodist theologian Frances Young is surely correct when she writes, "Christian thought about suffering cannot be reduced to explaining it away, in however philosophically sophisticated a way. It must rather embrace the fact that suffering lies at the heart of its formative story."[3] This is nowhere more obvious than in these words of the forsaken Jesus. Frances Young knows about suffering. She has a son named Arthur who has been severely disabled from birth, physically and mentally. She and her husband, Bob, have looked after their son for decades. They know the meaning of suffering.[4]

Earlier in chapter 15 of the Gospel, Jesus is on trial before Pilate. Asked by the Roman, "Are you the King of the Jews?" Jesus had replied, "You say so." There is no further word from Jesus in the passion narrative of St. Mark until we come to this word from the cross. Jesus is utterly silent. This particular cry of abandonment breaks the silence. The gospels are written in Greek. The very fact that Mark presents this word of Jesus in Aramaic, Jesus's own language, before he offers it to us in Greek suggests powerfully that this cry may be an actual, historical memory of Jesus's final agonized words. Perhaps someone who was there on Calvary may have remembered Jesus crying out these words.

The words "My God, my God, why have you forsaken me?" are a quotation from Psalm 22. Centuries before

2. Ibid., 122.
3. Young, "Suffering," 689.
4. Young, *Arthur's Call.*

Jesus used these words, they were penned by a poet as he went through some desolate experience. We don't know specifically what the psalmist's experience was, but we do know—he tells us—that he feels forsaken by God. This sense of being forsaken elicits from the suffering poet the question "Why?" God was silent in response to the psalmist's "why" and God is silent in response to Jesus's "why."[5]

The Roman community of the first century for whom Mark was probably writing also knew the cross and knew God's silence. There is a strong tradition that the Gospel of Mark was written in Rome just after the Emperor Nero had crucified many in the Christian community in 64 AD, the time when Peter and Paul met their deaths. The Roman historian Tacitus, no friend of the Christian movement, tells us that Nero then set fire to the crucified bodies on the Appian Way, a major road into Rome, for the entertainment of the citizens of the empire's capital. "Mark is writing for a church baffled and fearful because the signs and the miracles aren't coming thick and fast. What is coming thick and fast is persecution and a sense of threat and failure. Mark is writing in the life of communities experiencing fear and disorientation."[6] We might say that the Roman Christian community was on the cross every bit as much as Jesus had been. We might say that the Roman Christian community had made its own Jesus's cry of abandonment, "My God, my God, why have you forsaken us?" They must certainly have felt abandoned at this time.

"Darkness has covered the earth; there is nothing that shows God acting on Jesus' side. How appropriate that Jesus feel forsaken! His 'Why?' is that of someone who has

5. Radcliffe, *Seven Last Words*, 42.

6. Williams, *Meeting God in Mark*, 46.

plumbed the depths of the abyss, and feels enveloped by the power of darkness. Jesus is not questioning the existence of God or the power of God to do something about what is happening; he is questioning the silence of the one whom he calls 'My God.'"[7] Jesus is questioning the silence of God. God has no special word for him as he is asphyxiating on the cross. Brutalized by suffering, Jesus echoes the cry of everyone who suffers. People who suffer in the most agonizing of ways, especially when that suffering has nothing to do with anything they have done (innocent suffering), must wonder, "Why me? Why is this happening to me? Have I done something to bring this on myself?" And the answer is, "No!" There simply is no persuasive answer to the question why so much suffering has fallen on this person rather than that person. Pain and suffering are just the tragic consequences of the world in which we live. Pain and suffering are just the tragic consequences of the way things go in our fragile, physical, relational, weblike universe. Pain and suffering are also the way things go as a result of the poor moral choices we humans make.[8]

Could God have made a world free of pain and suffering? I think we have to say yes—the logic of the concept "God" seems to demand that. But God could not have made *this* world differently, this world in which we live. The laws of physics and chemistry and biology that govern our webbed world and produce vast vistas of inspiring beauty and grandeur are the same laws that bring about illness, pain, and suffering. The freedom with which God gifts us is such that its misuse on our part can lead to pain and suffering in others as well as ourselves, but we could

7. Brown, *Death of the Messiah*, 2:1046.

8. See Barton, *Love Unknown*, 17.

not find love without this two-edged sword that freedom is, and who would want to live in a flawless and perfect world without love? God did not predetermine that Jesus would have to suffer on the cross, just as God does not predetermine that any of us has to suffer on our own crosses. That would turn God into a cruel tyrant. What God did in the whole event of Jesus, in the incarnation and crucifixion, was to enter into the messy details of our world, a world marked by arbitrariness and unpredictability. The God who is nothing but unconditional Love, embodied and made visible in Jesus, lets the consequences of being Love in our flawed human world happen without evasion or avoidance.[9] He did not turn away from pain and suffering. Perhaps we could say that through Jesus, pain and suffering are absorbed into the life of God, and, if absorbed, then finally transformed.

Mark's Jesus dies in agony with a wordless cry—"Jesus gave a loud cry and breathed his last" (Mark 15:37). While the other evangelists soften the final moment of Jesus's death, Mark does nothing to relieve the "unadorned brutality" of the death of Jesus.[10] We know from the gospel tradition as a whole that Jesus's favored and customary address of God was "Abba, Father." Abba was an intimate form of address for one's father, a form of address that brings into sharp relief all those memories that shape and bond loving union between a father and a son. One of my grandchildren, three-year-old Finley, calls his father "Adda." For whatever reasons, Finley prefers "Adda" to "Dada." And, of course, that pleases me since it is so close to Jesus's customary "Abba." There is nothing of Jesus's

9. Ibid., 16–17.

10. Senior, *Jesus in the Gospel of Mark*, 125.

intimacy with Abba here. In this word from the cross, Jesus does not address God as "Abba, Father," but rather starkly as "My God." "Nowhere previously has Jesus ever prayed to God as 'God' . . . Feeling forsaken as if he were not being heard, he no longer presumes to speak intimately to the All-Powerful as 'Father' but employs the address common to all human beings, 'My God.'"[11]

If "My God" rather than "My Abba, my dear Father" has replaced Jesus's habitual address of God, then we can also feel the force of the word "Why?" in this saying of Jesus. It is a why that has reached the bottom of the pit of despair, and perhaps expects no answer. On the Calvary cross, there is no intelligible "Why." One is left simply with loving trust. When there is no intelligibility in the face of suffering and pain, when there is no point, gazing at the forsaken Christ on the crucifix may be the only way of loving trust.[12] This was the way of the medieval theologian Peter Abelard (1079–1142). While Abelard did not suffer horrendously as did Jesus or the early Roman Christians, his life and the choices he made brought much suffering on him. One theological commentator writes, "Paradoxically enough, this man, whose life was broken because of the tragic consequences of his love of Heloise, and whose theological career was lived out in the midst of a storm of controversy, became the greatest advocate of that interpretation of the work of Christ which sees it as supremely love enkindling love."[13] Abelard himself wrote, "He died for us to no other end than that true liberty of love might be propagated in us, through that loftiest love which He

11. Brown, *Death of the Messiah*, 2:1046.
12. Hume, *Hope from the Cross*, 42.
13. Culpepper, *Interpreting the Atonement*, 88.

displayed to us."[14] If absurdity in the face of suffering is not to have the last word, gazing with Abelard on the cross of Christ, love enkindling love, trusting love, is the only finally meaningful way.

14. Abelard, *Commentary* 5:5, quoted in Galloway, *Basic Readings in Theology*, 106.

7

The Fifth Word from the Cross

"I thirst."

The fifth word is taken from the Gospel according to John (19:28).

After this, aware that everything was now finished, in order that the scripture might be fulfilled, Jesus said, "I thirst."

What does Jesus mean by saying, "I thirst"? Reading the gospels backward is the best way to go if one wants to understand what Jesus meant.[1] Perhaps the best place to begin thinking about this passage is earlier in St. John's Gospel where Jesus has gone up to Jerusalem for the Festival of Booths, and on the last day of the festival he

1. I am echoing here the excellent book by New Testament scholar Richard B. Hays, *Reading Backwards.*

cried out, "Let anyone who is thirsty come to me, and let the one who believes in me drink. As the scripture has said, 'Out of the believer's heart shall flow rivers of living water'" (John 7:37–38). In this passage Jesus is the one who slakes our human thirst. Read back to an even earlier passage in John, to the conversation between Jesus and the Samaritan woman at the well (John 4). The conversation begins with Jesus asking this woman for a drink of water, but continues in this vein: "Those who drink of the water that I will give them will never be thirsty. The water that I will give will become in them a spring of water gushing up to eternal life" (John 4:14). Two things to note: Jesus is thirsty, and Jesus will slake human thirst beyond all imagining, so that those who drink from him will never thirst again.

Right now, in the context of the cross, perhaps those words "I thirst" could simply be a statement of fact, an expression of extreme thirst as he is dying, but the problem is that the Gospel of St. John is not much interested in matters of fact. John's interest is in symbolism. John writes on two levels: the level of the obvious, the surface meaning of the text, and the level of deeper, symbolic meaning. On this latter level St. John works especially through allusion to the Old Testament. So, let's read back to two passages from the Psalms, Psalms 22 and 42, which may serve as the allusions to this word from the cross, "I thirst." Here, also, St. John moves from the obvious and surface meaning to the deeper and more symbolic meaning.

The first Psalms passage is Psalm 22, the psalm considered earlier, in which the author cries out, "My God, my God, why have you forsaken me?" If we scroll down in this psalm to verse 15, there we read, "My mouth is dried up like a piece of pottery, and my tongue sticks to my jaws;

you lay me in the dust of death." "My mouth is dried up like a piece of pottery"—the psalmist is describing terrible thirst. Raymond Brown comments, "While thirst is not mentioned in the verse, clearly the sufferer suffers from it to the point of death." That is helpful. If Jesus meant his literal thirst because of his sufferings, the question emerges, why did St. John not quote this particular verse? It may be because the psalmist "is accusing God of having brought him to this situation, while John sees Jesus as the master of his fate."[2] Jesus on the cross in St. John's Gospel is no victim of circumstances. He is the director of the entire play that is his life, and most especially of this last act. He is in control. When the militia comes out to the Garden of Gethsemane to arrest him, he strides out to meet them, asking, "Whom are you looking for?": "They answered, 'Jesus of Nazareth.' Jesus replied, 'I am he' . . . When Jesus said to them 'I am he,' they stepped back and fell to the ground" (John 18:4–7). Jesus is in control of the situation. Even a cursory glance at his trial before Pontius Pilate suggests that it is really Pilate who is on trial, Pilate who asks, "What is truth?" (John 18:38). And so one is pushed to ask about a deeper meaning than the literal one of "I thirst."

That takes us to the second allusion, Psalm 42: "As a deer longs for flowing streams, so my soul longs for you, O God. My soul thirsts for God, for the living God" (42:1–2). The human soul of Jesus thirsts for God, the living God, because he knows that in God alone will his thirst be slaked. This is a constant theme in our Christian tradition. We have an innate orientation to the divine. Everyone has this orientation. We seek that which will finally and fully

2. Brown, *Death of the Messiah*, 2:1073.

satisfy all the longings of the human heart. Think of that famous line from St. Augustine's autobiography, in fact from the opening paragraph of his *Confessions*: "you have made us for yourself, and our heart is restless until it rests in you."[3] We humans thirst for God even if that which we thirst for is anonymous, unnamed. God may be known without necessarily being named.

Thus far, the meaning of "I thirst" turns on our human thirsting for God. The other side of the coin, as it were, is God's thirsting for us. "Most of all God wants us. Usually we think that reaching God is hard work. We must earn forgiveness; we must become good, otherwise he will disapprove of us. But this is wrong. God comes to us before we have ever turned to him. God thirsts for our love. He is racked with desire for us."[4] The Catechism of the Catholic Church puts it like this: "God thirsts for us that we might thirst for him."[5] In saying—better, "in proclaiming"—the words "I thirst," Jesus identifies with the thirst *of* God for every man, woman, and child. Equally, Jesus identifies with the thirst *for* God of every man, woman, and child. In chapter 1 of this Gospel we are told that Jesus is the Eternal Word of God through whom all creation came to be: "All things came into being through him, and without him not one thing came into being" (John 1:3). Jesus is the Eternal Creative Word, we may say, eternally thirsting for every one of his creatures. Now on the cross he is the Eternal Word paradoxically expiring out of this thirst. "I thirst for you, and you, for all, for everyone who exists and ever shall

3. Augustine, *Confessions*, 3.
4. Radcliffe, *Seven Last Words*, 49–50.
5. *Catechism of the Catholic Church*, no. 2560.

exist." God thirsts for every human being, no exception. Human beings thirst for God, no exception.

One of my all-time favorite authors is the fourteenth-century mystic and theologian Julian of Norwich. She wrote about God's thirst: "For as truly as there is in God a quality of pity and compassion, so is there in God a quality of thirst and longing. . . . And this quality of longing and thirst comes from God's everlasting goodness, just as the quality of pity comes from his everlasting goodness. . . . And this is the characteristic of spiritual thirst, which will persist in him so long as we are in need, and will draw us up into his bliss."[6] It is simply a most beautiful passage giving expression to God's love for us. However, notice the occurrence of the word "thirst." Julian is telling us that God thirsts for us. Julian was a medieval woman, and in medieval theology God has no needs. God is perfect and complete in himself. Julian is telling us, by way of contrast, that God thirsts and longs for us. Julian almost suggests that God is incomplete without us, and if God is incomplete without us, so is Jesus. We are incomplete, remaining thirsty without God, and God remains incomplete, thirsty, without us.

6. Julian of Norwich, *Showings*, Long Text 31, 231.

8

The Sixth Word from the Cross

"It is finished."

The sixth word is taken from the Gospel according to John (19:30).

There was a vessel filled with common wine. So they put a sponge soaked in wine on a sprig of hyssop and put it up to his mouth. When Jesus had taken the wine, he said, "It is finished."

"What Jesus literally says is, 'It is perfected.' At the beginning of the Last Supper, St. John tells us that 'having loved his own who were in the world, he loved them to perfection.' On the cross we see the perfection of love."[1] This is not so obvious. We need to think about it more. Jesus, having loved his own in this world—loved

1. Radcliffe, *Seven Last Words*, 57.

them "to the utmost extent"—it is no mere coincidence that the death on the cross follows so quickly upon Jesus's last supper. The last supper, the Eucharist, is *the* sign of this life-giving love. It is put so beautifully by Scripture scholar John Barton: "The broken bread and wine poured out are symbols of the total self-emptying and brokenness of the one who freely laid down his life because he freely embraced the lot of the whole human race, including—including above all—its helplessness and bondage to death and suffering. That is the kind of God to whom all who take his body and blood in the Eucharist are committing themselves; a God who will 'break his own heart to comfort ours,' and who offers us the chance to become people who will do the same for each other and, indeed, for the least of our brothers and sisters."[2] What a wonderful passage. Our Lovely God, rendered sacramentally for us in the eucharistic self-gift, invites us to break our hearts in love to comfort others.

"These words of Jesus invite us to carry on seeking to love perfectly. We will arrive at that fullness of love in the end and at the end."[3] Where that kind of love is present in our lives, even in our striving now, God is present because God is the Love that is the logic of the universe. Our hope is that this Love-Logic will play out in our lives until we come home to the Father's house.

That is not the thinking of Francis Underwood, president of the United States, in the series *House of Cards*. In one grotesque scene President Underwood walks into a Washington church. He approaches the large crucifix and speaks to the Crucified: "Love! That's what you're selling.

2. Barton, *Love Unknown*, 36.
3. Radcliffe, *Seven Last Words*, 58–59.

Well, I don't buy it." And he proceeds to spit on the corpus of Jesus. He attempts to wipe his spittle from the corpus, and it falls to the ground, smashed into a thousand pieces. Underwood is possessed of "overvaulting ambition," he is selfish, adulterous, mean-minded, nasty. He is a supreme narcissist. As the series unfolds, it becomes clear that President Underwood never felt loved by his father, and that fundamental lack of love has left him very broken.

Theologian Herbert McCabe is fully aware of the need of children to be loved and to feel love if they are to flourish as adults. McCabe writes,

> One thing that is necessary for the health and growth of children is that they should believe that their parents love them. This is almost as necessary as food and drink. . . . The whole of our faith is the belief that God loves us; I mean there isn't anything else. Anything else we say we believe is just a way of saying that God loves us. Any proposition, any article of faith, is only an expression of faith if it is a way of saying that God loves us. . . . God, for the Christian, is the lover who accepts us absolutely and unconditionally, quite regardless of whether we are nice or nasty. We put this simply by saying that God loves sinners. This is what the cross says, and that is why it is the center of Christian faith. God cannot fail to love us, whatever we do. But we can fail to believe this.[4]

President Underwood does not understand this, and likewise, too many of us fail to understand.

Sometimes the message of the cross is portrayed in other terms. Sometimes Christ's passion is viewed "as a

4. McCabe, *Faith Within Reason*, 33–35.

punitive blood sacrifice." I want to distance myself from that kind of unhelpful thinking. In that kind of punitive thinking, "God is seen . . . as vengeful and possessing an honor that is easily offended, not humble, not patient, not infinitely forgiving, in other words, a God *un*like the God consistently portrayed in Jewish and Christian Scripture. Only pain and blood sacrifice will do."[5] Jesus did not set out to be crucified as some kind of punishment for human sin. Jesus set out to be the visibility of God, rendering visible and audible and tactile the God who is nothing but Love. The disturbing event of Jesus, his teaching and his actions, was the expression of the Love that God is. That is what stirred up opposition to Jesus—the opposition that crucified him. His very presence fundamentally challenged those "who did not wish to change or to give up their power and privilege, and so Jesus encountered rejection, persecution, hostility, arrest, torture, and execution. Since Jesus lived in readiness for everything that his work and love of God would bring, he freely gave over his body, blood, mind, heart, and life for God and his people."[6] With these final words, "It is finished," we hear that the Love of God, which Jesus is visibly, has now reached the point beyond which in human terms it cannot go, the point of death. "He loved his own in the world and he loved them to the end."

In another sense, however, it is not finished until it is finished in each of us. The Jewish philosopher Emmanuel Levinas (1906–95) helps us understand something of how "it is not finished until it is finished in each of us." Levinas writes, "The face is the way in which the other presents

5. Callahan, *Created for Joy*, 78.
6. Ibid., 88–89.

himself to me."[7] The issue is my response to the other. The only adequate way to respond to the face of the other is to say, "Here I am. What can I do to help?" Developing this line of thought, we may say that responding to the face of the other is responding to the Face of the Other. In saying to the Divine Other met in the human other, "Here I am. What can I do to help?" I am letting the words of Jesus find their home in me. It is not finished until it is finished in me. The self-emptying of Love that is Jesus—he loved his own *eis telos*, "to the finish," "to the end"—now passes over into us who follow this Jesus. This self-emptying love, this responding to the face of the other/Other, brings into play the words of Jesus in Matthew 25: "Truly, I say to you, as you did it to one of the least of these my brethren, you did it to me" (25:40). The self-emptying love for others is finished for the body of the historic Jesus on the cross, but the "finishing" of this self-emptying love remains the lifelong challenge of all those who dare to call themselves the Body of Christ in this world.

7. Levinas, *Totality and Infinity*, 50, slightly altered.

9

The Seventh Word from the Cross

"Father, into your hands I commend my spirit."

The seventh word is taken from the Gospel according to Luke (23:44–46).

It was now about noon and darkness came over the whole land until three in the afternoon because of an eclipse of the sun. Then the veil of the temple was torn down the middle. Jesus cried out in a loud voice, "Father into your hands I commend my spirit." And when he had said this, he breathed his last.

The great Jesuit priest-poet Gerard Manley Hopkins (1844–89) died of typhoid in Dublin, Ireland, where he was Professor of Greek at University College Dublin.

The Dying of Jesus

His Jesuit confreres surrounding him on his deathbed heard him say two or three times, "I am so happy, I am so happy."[1] The significance of Hopkins's last words comes to clarity when we recall that he suffered from what today would be diagnosed as clinical depression. This depression emerges in what have been called his "terrible sonnets," one of which begins with these difficult words:

> I wake and feel the fell of dark, not day.
> What hours, O what black hours we have spent
> This night![2]

Jesus on the cross felt "the fell of dark, not day." He knew, from the time of his agony in the Garden of Gethsemane until his dying moment, what Hopkins meant by the words, "What hours, O what black hours we have spent this night!" In this final word from St. Luke, however, we get no sense of this darkness, or these black hours of the night.

Jesus does not die in St. Luke's Gospel with that dreadful cry, "My God, my God, why have you abandoned me?" Luke softens Jesus's words. He uses a different word than does St. Mark; he chooses the verb "to cry out" (*phonein*) in preference to Mark's "scream" (*boan*). As in Mark so in Luke the dying Jesus prays words from a psalm, in this case Psalm 31:5: "Into your hand I commit my spirit." The words of the psalmist are not the words of a man facing into his death. They are the words of one entrusting his life to "God's safekeeping. He does so in confidence because all that he knows of God from past experience

---

1. White, *Hopkins*, 455.
2. Hopkins, *Poems and Prose*, 62.

points him in this direction."[3] The psalmist has experienced the faithfulness of God throughout his life and so in the context of this psalm he reaffirms that trust. The psalmist has "the confident hope that he will be delivered from his present affliction."[4] The difference between the Hebrew psalmist, who prays with trust and confidence in God, and Jesus is this: the psalmist is committing his life to God, Jesus is committing his death to God. Jesus's experience of his Abba points him like the psalmist in this direction of trusting confidence in God, but now for Jesus a trusting confidence in God in the face of his immediate dying and death. The darkness is there, the darkness of an excruciating death. But he does not scream into the darkness. "Luke has created a different mood. Even though the powers of darkness seem triumphant, Jesus dies confidently, entrusting his spirit into the hands of his Father. The power of darkness has been defeated by Jesus' trust in a faithful God."[5]

St. Luke also wrote the book known as the Acts of the Apostles, and there we read of Stephen, stoned to death outside Jerusalem. Like his Lord and Master, Stephen forgives those who are killing him: "Lord, do not hold this sin against them" (7:60)—a paraphrase of Jesus on the cross praying, "Father, forgive them; for they do not know what they are doing" (Luke 23:24). And, like Jesus once again, Stephen prays, "Lord Jesus, receive my spirit" (7:59). St. Luke is teaching us how to die with trustful confidence like Jesus, like Stephen. Like so many of those who have gone before us marked with the sign of faith.

3. Davidson, *Vitality of Worship*, 107.
4. Weiser, *Psalms*, 276.
5. Senior, *Jesus in the Gospel of Luke*, 144.

Think, for example, of the eighty-six-year-old Poly-carp (ca. 69–156), bishop of Smyrna, who was burned to death. Refusing to acknowledge the genius of Caesar, the divinity of the Roman emperor, he prays at his horrendous death, "Lord God almighty, father of thy blessed and be-loved Son Jesus Christ . . . may I be received among them [the martyrs] this day in thy presence."[6] Polycarp entrusted himself to the loving hands of God. This word of Jesus, "Into your hands I commend my spirit," may be a mouth-piece for us when all our experiences of pain and sorrow and the final pain of death come our way. Like Jesus we can say, "Into your hands I commend my spirit." These words do not deny the reality of our pain and suffering, nor do they express some kind of joy in pain and suffering. Denial and joy in such contexts are unreal. Both denial and joy in pain do violence to us. "We are not made for pain; we are made for happiness."[7] Paradoxically, we may find the hap-piness we seek in the trusting confidence of Jesus ("Into your hands I commend my spirit"). Or, in the very differ-ent context of the dying Gerard Manley Hopkins, "I am so happy." Dying into the hands of our Lovely God inspires a certain happiness, or certainly hope-filled confidence.

It is reported that among the last words of author and religious journalist Peter Hebblethwaite (1930–94), as he was nearing death in his home in Oxford, were: "Ma-ranatha. Come, Lord Jesus."[8] What a beautiful way for a Christian to leave this world. The last words of Irish poet and Nobel laureate Seamus Heaney, addressed to his wife minutes before his death on August 30, 2013, were: "*Noli*

6. Staniforth and Louth, *Early Christian Writings*, 129–30.

7. Hume, *Hope from the Cross*, 71.

8. Fox, "Peter Hebblethwaite," 2.

timere—don't be afraid."[9] There is something fearful about dying and death. It's only natural to be somewhat afraid—afraid of the literally unknown. That's part of what makes Heaney's words so inspiring. As he faced this lonely passage, his thoughts went out to his wife of many years to comfort her: "Don't be afraid."

On March 13, 2015, a friend of mine died, the Benedictine monk Fr. Paschal Cheline. As he prepared for the moment of death, he used that 1889 poem by Alfred Lord Tennyson, "Crossing the Bar." The poem is about crossing the sandbar of death as the ship of one's life moves out toward the great untraveled ocean of death:

> For tho' from out our bourne of Time and Place
>> The flood may bear me far,
> I hope to see my Pilot face to face
>> When I have crossed the bar.

Meeting one's Pilot face to face is Tennyson's way of saying with the Lord, "Father, into your hands I commend my spirit."

Father Karl Rahner, arguably the most influential Catholic theologian of the twentieth century and a great composer of prayers, puts "into your hands I commend my spirit" like this: "Those hands are so gentle and so sure. They are like the hands of a mother . . . and the Motherly Father will kiss away the tears from the cheeks of his Son. O Jesus, will you one day put my poor soul and my poor life into these gentle hands of your Father?"[10]

9 McDonald, "Seamus Heaney's Last Words," para. 2.

10. Adapted from Rahner, *Prayers for a Lifetime*, 58–59.

Bibliography

Abbott, Walter M., and Joseph Gallagher, eds. *The Documents of Vatican II*. New York: Guild, 1966.

Andreopoulos, Andreas. *The Sign of the Cross: The Gesture, the Mystery, the History*. Brewster, MA: Paraclete, 2006.

Augustine, St. *Confessions*. Translated by Henry Chadwick. New York: Oxford University Press, 1992.

Barton, John. *Love Unknown: Meditations on the Death and Resurrection of Jesus*. London: SPCK, 1990.

Beattie, Tina. *Rediscovering Mary: Insights from the Gospels*. Liguori, MO: Triumph Books, 1995.

Brown, Raymond E. *The Death of the Messiah: From Gethsemane to the Grave; a Commentary on the Passion Narratives in the Four Gospels*. 2 vols. Garden City, NY: Doubleday, 1994.

Burtchaell, James T. *Philemon's Problem*. Grand Rapids: Eerdmans, 2001.

Callahan, Sidney. *Created for Joy: A Christian View of Suffering*. New York: Crossroad, 2007.

Cross, Frank L. *The Early Christian Fathers*. London: G. Duckworth, 1960.

Culpepper, Robert H. *Interpreting the Atonement*. Grand Rapids: Eerdmans, 1966.

Cummings, Owen F. *Eucharistic Doctors: A Theological History*. New York: Paulist, 2005.

———. "The Grace of Graham Greene (1904–1991)." In *Thinking About Prayer*, 65–76. Eugene, OR: Wipf and Stock, 2009.

Bibliography

———. "Graham Greene and Monsignor Quixote's Final Eucharist." In *Eucharist and Ecumenism: The Eucharist across the Ages and Traditions*, 124–31. Eugene, OR: Pickwick, 2013.

———. "Sacraments of Initiation and Reconciliation." In *Exploring Theology: Making Sense of the Catholic Tradition*, edited by Anne Hession et al., 242–49. Dublin: Veritas, 2007.

Davidson, Robert. *The Vitality of Worship*. Grand Rapids: Eerdmans, 1998.

Donne, John. *The Sermons of John Donne*. Edited by George R. Potter and Evelyn M. Simpson. Vol. 4. Berkeley: University of California Press, 1959.

Ford, David F. *The Shape of Living*. London: HarperCollins, 1997.

Fox, Thomas C. "Peter Hebblethwaite Wrote of Church He Knew, Loved." *National Catholic Reporter*, January 6, 1995, 2.

Galloway, Allan D., ed. *Basic Readings in Theology*. Cleveland: World, 1964.

Gaventa, Beverly. *Mary: Glimpses of the Mother of Jesus*. Columbia: University of South Carolina Press, 1995.

Greene, Graham. *Monsignor Quixote*. New York: Simon and Schuster, 1982.

Hare, Douglas R. A. *Matthew*. Louisville: John Knox, 1992.

Harrington, Daniel. *Jesus: A Historical Portrait*. Cincinnati: St. Anthony Messenger Press, 2007.

Hauerwas, Stanley. *Cross-Shattered Christ: Meditations on the Last Seven Words*. Grand Rapids: Brazos, 2004.

Hays, Richard B. *Reading Backwards: Figural Christology and the Fourfold Gospel Witness*. Waco: Baylor University Press, 2014.

Hengel, Martin. *The Atonement: The Origins of the Doctrine in the New Testament*. Philadelphia: Fortress, 1981.

Herbert, George. *The Complete English Poems*. Edited by John Tobin. New York: Penguin, 1991.

Hopkins, Gerard Manley. *Poems and Prose of Gerard Manley Hopkins*. Selected by W. H. Gardner. New York: Penguin, 1985.

Houselander, Caryll. *The Way of the Cross*. New York: Sheed and Ward, 1955.

Hume, Basil. *Hope from the Cross: Reflections on Jesus' Seven Last Words*. Edited by Liam Kelly. Frederick, MD: The Word Among Us, 2009.

Jeanrond, Werner G. *Call and Response: The Challenge of Christian Life*. New York: Continuum, 1995.

Julian of Norwich. *Showings*. Translated by Edmund Colledge and James Walsh. New York: Paulist, 1978.

Bibliography

Lake, Kirsopp, trans. *The Apostolic Fathers.* 2 vols. New York: Macmillan, 1912–13.

Levinas, Emmanuel. *Totality and Infinity: An Essay on Exteriority.* Translated by Alphonso Lingis. Pittsburgh: Duquesne University Press, 1969.

Macquarrie, John. *Paths in Spirituality.* 2nd ed. Harrisburg, PA: Morehouse, 1992.

Martini, Carlo Maria. *Journeying with the Lord: Reflections for Every Day.* New York: Alba House, 1987.

McCabe, Herbert. *Faith Within Reason.* Edited by Brian Davies. London: Continuum, 2007.

McDonald, Henry. "Seamus Heaney's Last Words Were 'Noli timere,' Son Tells Funeral." *The Guardian,* September 2, 2013, http://www.theguardian.com/books/2013/sep/02/seamus-heaney-last-words-funeral.

Neuhaus, Richard J. *Death on a Friday Afternoon: Meditations on the Last Words of Jesus from the Cross.* New York: Basic Books, 2000.

Nouwen, Henri. *Walk With Jesus: Stations of the Cross.* Maryknoll, NY: Orbis, 1990.

O'Faolain, Nuala. *Are You Somebody? The Accidental Memoir of a Dublin Woman.* New York: Henry Holt, 1996.

Radcliffe, Timothy. *Seven Last Words.* London: Burns and Oates, 2004.

———. *Stations of the Cross.* Collegeville, MN: Liturgical, 2015.

Rahner, Karl. *Prayers for a Lifetime.* New York: Crossroad, 1995.

Sartre, Jean-Paul. *Being and Nothingness.* Translated by Hazel E. Barnes. New York: Washington Square, 1993.

Schoedel, William R. *Ignatius of Antioch.* Edited by Helmut Koester. Philadelphia: Fortress, 1985.

Senior, Donald. *The Passion of Jesus in the Gospel of Luke.* Wilmington: M. Glazier, 1989.

———. *The Passion of Jesus in the Gospel of Mark.* Wilmington: M. Glazier, 1984.

———. *Why the Cross?* Nashville: Abingdon, 2014.

Sherry, Patrick. *Images of Redemption: Art, Literature, and Salvation.* London: T. & T. Clark, 2003.

Spretnak, Charlene. *Missing Mary.* New York: Palgrave Macmillan, 2004.

Staniforth, Maxwell, and Andrew Louth, eds. *Early Christian Writings.* Rev. ed. New York: Penguin, 1989.

Viladesau, Richard. *The Beauty of the Cross: The Passion of Christ in Theology and the Arts, from the Catacombs to the Eve of the Renaissance.* New York: Oxford University Press, 2006.

Bibliography

Weiser, Artur. *The Psalms: A Commentary.* Translated by Herbert Hartwell. Philadelphia: Westminster, 1962.

White, Norman. *Hopkins: A Literary Biography.* Oxford: Clarendon, 1992.

Williams, Rowan D. *Meeting God in Mark.* London: SPCK, 2014.

Young, Frances M. *Arthur's Call.* London: SPCK, 2014.

———. "Suffering." In *The Oxford Companion to Christian Thought*, edited by Adrian Hastings et al., 689–90. New York: Oxford University Press, 2000.

Young, Frances M., with Andrew Teal. *From Nicaea to Chalcedon: A Guide to the Literature and Its Background.* 2nd ed. Grand Rapids: Baker Academic, 2010.

Stray

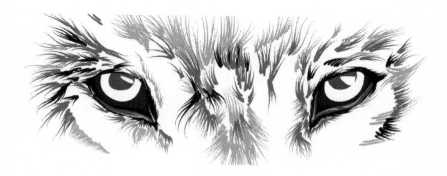

To Jurdae

Enjoy

Smokey Morrow

A

Smokey Moment

Novel

This book is fiction based on the imagination of the writer. Names, characters, places and incidents are creations of the writer for entertainment purposes and any resemblance to actual people, living or deceased, is purely coincidental.